Water solstice

Lindsey Huebner

BookLeaf Publishing

Presentation by *BookLeaf Publishing*

Web: www.bookleafpub.com

E-mail: info@bookleafpub.com

ISBN: 9789357441735

First edition 2023

DEDICATION

To my mother, for sharing her love of words.

To my father, for unending support.

To James, and forging forevers one moment at a time.

ACKNOWLEDGEMENT

I am incredibly grateful for BookLeaf for the challenge. 21 Poems in 21 Days kicked my butt, but also opened up a new frontier of personal possibility. If you also tend toward inaction ("contemplation", as I like to call it), take the plunge- whatever your plunge might be; you'll be glad you did.

I am grateful to every person who planted and nurtured the seeds that writing is a thing I could actually do. Not because I'm great at it, but because creative expression is in itself a gift, and one we can give ourselves every day.

Solstice

I was promised the aurora
So I refused to love the stars.
But auspicious things begin in darkness
Or so I'm told.
Or so I'm told…

The crunch and squeak
Of snow beneath my feet
Through hollow landscapes.
I'm so far away
I echo
            echo

                    Echo.

(What were we fighting about again?)

Silence crescendos
Listen:

Listen…

There is a fullness here
My foreign feet
Come home
At last
We are home
Rest your weary soul
In weary boots
My, how the journey changed us all.

The darkness that I dread comes so soon
But we have reached the turning point:
From now on, there will be light,
From now on, there will be light.
From now on, there will be light!

We have learned our sunless lessons
And surely this time will be different
Surely.

Surely.
Surely

Trickster

The trickster beholds these humourless lands
With their humourless humans
With their humourless gods
Guffawless,
Barely a chortle whispering through the
all-too-serious leaves,
And says with a snort and a fart,
"Bit shit, innit?"

Can't say I disagree.

I mourn my heretical mythologies:
My Loki, my Whiskey Jack, my Monkey God,
my Pan, my Anansi,
(My joy, my cheekiness, my peevishness, my
profanity, my humanity)
Those whose names we've long forgotten,
Those humiliated by white men on white clouds,
Terrified of what might be forged deep in gut's
laughter,
Terrified of the solace it might unearth,
Terrified that terror may not be life's only
solace,
Terrified.

I pray to them
Knowing full-well their blood is not mine
And that I have been complicit in their
destruction
They laugh at my self-flagellation
As they should
As I should
I think myself too serious for their grace
But I am hopeful all the same.

Still Life

Imagine this
Imagine this
A he
A she
Their shared abyss
The gulf between
Is held and still
An inspiration
Stubborn force of will
Then suffocation
Will ensue
Unless a bridge is made
And it is true
That pride prevents
these separate stars
within their spheres
Coming together
But it is clear
Although they appear
No more separate than finger and thumb
Their distance is lightyears
And no more can come together
Than collide the sun
With her nearest celestial kin.

An exhalation
The invitation
But no movement is seen
Neither here nor there
Caught in between
Liminal spaces
Liminal hearts
Liminal faces
Liminal arts
Surely there is movement deep within
But for now, no yielding
One cannot let the other win.

Imagine this
Imagine this
A she
A he
Their shared abyss
Words hang between them
Suspended in space
Words unspoken
And those they would erase.

Alien

Every so often
I make the choice
To wander these lands
And watch my kind
As the outsider might
And I could choose to observe
The ugly lines drawn and re-drawn upon
windswept sand
And arbitrary pigmentation determining destiny
I could watch the hoarding of the few and the
scarcity of the many
I could watch the disregard for any life that
looks different from ours;

Instead,
I make the choice
To wander these lands
And watch my kind
As the outsider might
Observing
The hundreds of fragrant apples stacked high on
supermarket shelves
The soft steam from my coffee dancing and
dissolving into the morning air
The miracle of plants and all they give to life

The paper-bound ideas that we can decode
The forbidden glances and half-smiles of
strangers on the tube
The unguarded laughter of the baby in her pram
The now so-common devices with everyone I've
ever known
Available with a swipe of my thumb.

The unlikelihood of the spoken word
The unlikelihood of understanding the spoken
words of another
The impossible symphony of the human body
And all its systems
Somehow resulting in a singular self
A thing we call "I"
Distinct and unimaginably intrinsic to the whole.

Two steps back
One might see
The objective beauty
So easily missed
While living in this holy mess.

a loaf of bread

Unassuming
Steaming and enticing
Round and brown
Fluffy, fragrant and oh so fresh
Life giving and chokka with the evils of the day
Enemy to waistlines and diabetics everywhere
Moreish
Succulent
Saliva forming
Stretchy, bouncy
Glutinous, Gluten-ous,
Joyous
Melting my butter
Melting in my mouth
Melting my mouth
Melting me
And so, so simple

Life's too short for bad bread.

meditation i

Come on stillness
Work your magic!
…

…

…

    Stillness?

        Helloooo?

The virtuous are still
High-performers are still
Inanimate objects are still
I'm still still

You promised everything in your nothing
So here I am:
Still as fuck.
(Where's my prize?)
…

Okay, I'm breathing.
(Does that count?)
I'm not intentionally moving, but a gal's gotta
breathe, right?
You wouldn't want me dead, right? Right?!
Not here on the precipice of nirvana -

Or whatever the heck it is we're after.

…

THERE IS NO POETRY HERE
JUST A WASTE OF TIME

…

Come oooooooon, I'm still!
Super super still.
The still-est.

…

Okay, I'm thinking.
(Surely that doesn't count!)
Gal's gotta think, right?
I think therefore I am, right?
And if there's one thing I know I know
It's that I am
And therefore I think
I am
Therefore

…

…

…

…

I'm bored.

I love you like salt

Oh sweet one
How my skin prickles and reaches
At the sight of you
I hear the charged air fizz and pop
And I think, rather fondly,
We did that.
That was us.
You emptied your pockets
And presented your broken gifts
Or so you thought
What I received was starlight
And a shard of the eternal
No take-backs.
My salt love is yours
And I'll be emptying my own holey pockets
Until the end of my days
Finding divine trinkets
To keep you smiling.

fresh cement

imbued by the scattered impressions of others
like
    leaves
on
       fresh
   cement
leaving a print
but never deeper
than the beautiful reminder
that once there was life
that once there was death
and
   in
     the
      falling
Are we made permanent.

A case for immobility

Take a step:

.

Doors shut.

.

Paths fade.

.

The self narrows.

.

So defiantly -
I plant my feet and sneer at Possibility
And its audacious trespass.

.

I shall affect the sexy apathy,
That keeps me distant,
But oh so comfortable,
And oh so cool,

.

Some day they'll write stories about the person I
could have been.

meditation ii

I don't want to I don't want to I don't want to I'm
doing it
I don't I'm-
…
…
Ahhhh…
I see:

So this is where you've always been?

All your searching
All your scrambling
And my glasses perched proudly upon my brow
All this time

…

I am breathing
I am still
I am- no
Fuck it.
Lost it.
Fuck.

I'm hungry.

Words I like

petrichor, effervescent, melancholy, spume,
flume, ricochet, buffet, alight, frenetic, kinetic,
culpable, inculcate, Pollyanna, niceties, sonder,
flounder, drastic, nostalgia, insignia, ferreted,
extenuating, extricate, proprioception, emblem,
totem, squander, I LOVE YOU, fuck, cunt,
meander, indelible, fortuitous, circumspect,
radical, infinite, lacerate, Byzantine, entropy,
scoliosis, scythe, wring, melody, sonorous,
cacophony, calamitous, restitution, philanderer,
fetch, schematic, semantic, fecund, racketeer,
seminary, luminary, wine, beer, audacious,
salacious, sonata, fugue, felicity, vegan,
antiquity, cranial, parabola, bubble, rubble,
mellow, fellow

Overheard at the Tate Modern

"I can't decide if this is genius or bullshit."

Liquid Memoir

A liquid fills its container
So dutifully I flow
And there is room enough for me in me
What ever will I do with all this space?
The bubble breath caught in my lockdown throat
I choke on the words never formed by chapped lips
Their timid torrent is beautiful
Tribute and tributary to somber silence
Foam and flow from palate to teeth's tips
I whisper spume and starlight
Still and smooth as glass
I cannot wait to dip my oar in
Palpating perfection
The body knows, you know.

Time's Soliloquy

TIME: You may now think you know my
changeable face
When all you have perceived is but a fragment -
A simple construct, purpose-built to help
Discern in the simultaneousness
of existence: a Self.
This said, it is here possible for us
To leap between potentialities-
Which to me seem here but a single point.
Do not concern yourselves with logistics:
For to do so would undermine the play;
Instead take satisfaction in the fact
That this ability we have - and will
Now use to most dramatical effect.
In one eventuality Hermione lives;
Within the other: awaits she judgment or
redemption
She lingers in a place twixt there and here.
Dance we between the lines of that which is
And that which might or might not be.
And unto Purgatory I do transport thee.

Prey Creatures

Fearful, furtive, frozen, flighty/

Sounds imperceptible /
Smells aggressive and strange/

Pupils dilating/
The nervous system, prickly and fizzing/
You become your environment to survive/
We're not so different you and I/
What a miracle we are alive.

Fond, fun, fanciful, fickle and full,
There is no reason for your joy,
And yet your elation persists,
Buoyant hops and twists,
When reason urges you to run and to hide,
You are here, defiant in your relentless cheer,
We're not so different you and I,
What a miracle: we are alive.

Stream of Consciousness

Water. You can't have a stream without water. There is flow. Which is perhaps a quality and perhaps a sense. What in us perceives flow? Flow to what? Flow from where? What does it look like in another? I read that balance - or perhaps proprioception - is a sense - that of the self in space - and one so taken for granted it is largely disregarded. Like learning a language: we cannot forget once we know. Unless perhaps there's alcohol involved. That's a different kind of fire-water... Where was I? What happens when your inner ear solidifies and the body forgets? A toddler once again... I wonder if there is a person for every situation imaginable. If you can dream it, it has happened before and will happen again. Unless we persist in destroying the world as we know it. Surely an end to space brings about an end to us brings about an end to time? If no one is there to perceive it, does time exist? Tree falls in a forest, etc. etc. Immortality is gained by the extinction of those who perceive in the third dimension. Easy peasy! There's something in that... I don't think of myself as a morbid person. I know there's a touch of the poetic melancholy in me, but for the record I'll choose life every time. And for there to be life, there must be an ending to life. At least as we know it. I'm open to learning… Change is inevitable. I look to water for solace. It shows the path.

New year, new me.

Oh, happy, happy eve
Could be any other
But this, a mother
Of invention
Or co-creator
Artistic director
Of artistic directions
Differing, diverging-
I suppose what I'm saying is
We want different things
I want something
And you, you
Want nothing at all-
That's different, you see.
Reaching is all I want from you,
Beseeching of you the things I refuse to give
myself.
New Year-
Because we decided it so.
We created time and organised it in sections
Ordained by circles and stars
Instead of heartbeats and daylight and darkness.
Just as well.
Its spinning upon an axis dictates finality

And requires us to honour the conclusion of a
shared delusion.
Rebirth is the refrain;
Death the coda-
We are suspended in song
Contained within magnetic oppositions
Whose hum and thrum compose sweet melodies.

Pets.

Her position would be alarming
If I did not know better
She is at ease
She feels safe
I have earned this
Flopped on one side
Eyes half-closed
Little breaths
Little twitches
Little heartbeats
Cute as heck
How horrifying
I should give so much of my love
To something so small
And so vulnerable.

An inevitable heartbreak
Will never stop me loving.

Moonrise

'Til break of dawn
Without a yawn
Play we with lingering Moon
Our bodies two
But me and you
Shall weather sunrise soon

When Sun awakes
Away she takes
The magic of the night
Our tangled song
Awake is gone
Our moon has taken flight

Now dawn has broken
The Sun awoken
Half yawns and bleary eyes
But we do know
Where we shall go
When again our Moon does rise.

Insight Timer

Ten minutes was an eternity
In the stillness
With nothing to pass time
But thrumming caffeine heartbeats
And buzzing neural connections
A symphony of self
In anything but silence
Ten minutes was forever
Most often bargained away for quick fixes
Hacked by encoded biologies and algorithms
A choice I never made
I am not a computer,
Right?
I am not a computer-
I just behave like one at times.
Ten minutes is a whisper
Ten minutes can fundamentally alter your brain
chemistry
Ten minutes can be misplaced and never missed
Ten minutes can change your life
Ten minutes is a snooze

Every thing you've ever done was a collection of
minutes.

meditation iii

27

...
......
...
....
...
......
...

......

...

......

...

....

....

....

....

www.ingramcontent.com/pod-product-compliance
Lightning Source LLC
La Vergne TN
LVHW021335200726
843509LV00014B/2545